GRATITUDE

A Daily Journal for Busy Women

Boost Your Joy and Well-being, While Increasing
Your Capacity to Give and Receive.

Katherine Elizabeth Long
Foreword By: Kim Lenar-Ehrhardt

The publisher and author make no guarantees concerning the level of success you may experience by following the advice and strategies container in this book, and you accept the risk that results will differ for each individual. Testimonials provided are not intended to represent or guarantee that you will achieve the same or similar results.

This book does not replace the advice of a medical professional.
If you or someone you know is experiencing suicidal thoughts or crisis, please reach out to the Suicide Prevention Lifeline at 800-273-8255 or text HOME to the Crisis Text Line at 741741. These services are free and confidential.

Exploring Paths™ Publishing

www.exploringpathspublishing.com

Copyright © 2023, 2024 Katherine Elizabeth Long

All rights reserved. This book or any portion thereof may not be reproduced or used in any manner whatsoever without the publisher's express written permission except for using brief quotations in a book review.

Printed by Exploring Paths™ Publishing in the United States of America.

First printing, 2023.

Exploring Paths™ Publishing
12 Gay Road #1306
East Hampton, NY 11937

FORWARD

I am a gratitude journal hoarder. I don't know what it is, but a pretty journal always gets me. I'll put it next to my bed, full of good intentions and I might even manage a page or two and then I forget, I procrastinate and just don't do it.

At least that was the case before I met Katherine. First, my brain went into the typical "yeah, yeah, journaling your thoughts is healthy, but who has time for that"-mode, but listening to Katherine's story, hearing how and why she started publishing the journals, and learning about the scientific effect this framework has on our brains and overall health, changed my mind.

Could I have just gone back to one of the books I already own? Of course. But being given the chance to publish this version together with Katherine for women just like me, for busy moms and solopreneurs, and for the amazing members in our Hamptons BossMoms' community, makes it even more special and close to my heart. So here we are!

I really hope this journal will bring you as much joy and growth as it has brought me. If we help you change just one habit and shift your mindset just a tiny bit - it has already done what we are hoping it will do.

Let's do this. Together.

With Gratitude, Appreciation & Love,
Kim Lenar-Ehrhardt
Former Television and Media Executive & Founder of
TheKim.Code and Hamptons BossMoms

Katherine's Story

My journey through a challenging health crisis, the loss of jobs, relationships, the loss of a dear friend and cousin, and the loss of my father is a story of resilience, hope, and the power of gratitude. It offers insights for others navigating challenging paths where you may feel helpless, out of energy, overwhelmed, or alone.

Being diagnosed with a brain aneurysm at the age of 35 was one of the most significant life challenges I had faced. It was a rollercoaster of emotions, from disbelief and fear to eventual relief and gratitude. My experience, marked by misdiagnoses and dismissal, underscores the importance of trusting one's instincts and advocating for oneself, but also the unknown, the frustration, the fear, and the helplessness that comes with facing a new, taxing, and unknown challenge. The diagnosis was a turning point, bringing clarity amidst confusion and introducing new challenges.

My path, though fraught with challenges, was illuminated by my parents' wisdom: to always seek out the good in every situation. This mindset wasn't just a coping mechanism; it became a transformative force, teaching me the immense power of gratitude amidst adversity.

To women out there, my message is clear and heartfelt: prioritize self-care, find joy in small moments, and cherish time with loved ones. As a patient, daughter, sister, career woman, founder, and survivor, I want and need you to take time for yourself and keep doing things you love. Not only are you shouldering your own burdens, but you are also shouldering the burdens of those around you. The stress that accompanies putting yourself last is immense, though the mental fortitude to shift into a place of well-being is easily achievable with a few minutes of practice each day. I offer my story as a beacon of hope and encouragement.

This journal is a testament to my journey and is designed to guide you in finding strength through reflection and gratitude. It serves as a reminder that even in the most challenging times, there is a community of support and understanding ready to uplift and inspire.

With Love and Gratitude,
Katherine

*I have the
COURAGE
to make healthy
changes.*

Introduction

Perseverance is not a long race; it is many short races, one after the other. —Walter Elliot

As women, we embody immense beauty, strength, and complexity. We gracefully juggle countless roles—as caregivers, nurturers, career women, problem solvers, homemakers, wives, mothers, daughters, sisters, and friends. Our capacity to love and support others seems boundless. Yet, in our devotion to others, we often minimize our own needs. The daily stress of caring for those around us can quietly accumulate until our health suffers, directly impacting our desires and those around us.

Our own growth and fulfillment should not fall by the wayside. We, as women, have the power to break this cycle. We must challenge the notion that self-care is selfish or indulgent and give ourselves permission to prioritize our mental, physical, and emotional well-being. By setting boundaries and making space for self-reflection, we are taking time to refill our own cups. That, in turn, allows us to become the best versions of ourselves. We are able to serve ourselves and others from a place of abundance rather than depletion. When we care for ourselves first, we can approach our many goals, responsibilities, and desires with renewed energy and purpose.

And this is where we come in. Welcome you to *Gratitude: A Busy Woman's Journal*. Katherine, Kim, and LongeviSHE are thrilled to partner on this journal for the LongeviSHE community. Katherine and Exploring Paths Publishing's proven framework will guide you in prioritizing your mental, emotional, and physical well-being so you can nurture your best self.

Life often sweeps us up in obligations to others, leaving us depleted. We may feel guilty taking time for ourselves. But refilling our own cups allows us to share from abundance rather than scarcity. When you care for your inner self you can better weather storms and light the way for those around you. We owe it to ourselves and all who rely on us to make our well-being a priority.

You may be experiencing many feelings and wondering if this practice will help. The answer is a resounding YES.

By investing a fraction of your time and energy to focus on this workbook, you are recharging yourself, shifting your mindset towards solutions, and changing the environment around you. In return, you give yourself back the ability to focus on what is essential in your life and your role in caring for those around you.

As women, we create daily "to-do" lists and routines, and it is easy to fall into the trap of wanting to check all the boxes before we do anything for ourselves. That said, it is essential to remember the rule that flight attendants always tell us:

> "Put your oxygen mask on first before helping others."

This rule applies in life. Reflection, goal-setting, and gratitude practices are scientifically proven practices that will provide you with the oxygen you need to accomplish all that you desire; this journal is the mask to ensure you receive it.

In the next few pages, we will walk you through the key tenants of this workbook and their importance. So come along with us!

The Power of Reflection:

"We do not learn from experience... We learn from reflecting on experience" – John Dewey.

It sometimes feels easier to avoid or do nothing, though research shows that most people's biggest regrets are NOT taking "the" chances or initiatives. Daily reflection helps ensure we check in on ourselves and our needs consistently; it helps us with emotional regulation, increased self-awareness, learning and growth, and improved problem-solving and social connections. It makes sense. When we take the time to reflect on situations and circumstances, it forces us to go inward and look at alternatives and make sure that we are aligned with who we are and want to be.

At the same time, avoiding reflection and 'focusing on others' needs over our own' is an easy and addictive trap that is hazardous to our health. It allows built-up emotional and mental stress to wreak havoc on our minds, immune systems, and bodies. Furthermore, research has identified that once we establish a bad behavior, even unconsciously (like avoiding self-care), individuals can repeat those on autopilot even if they are mistakes.

Making time for yourself, if you haven't before, is starting a new healthy habit. It will take time and persistence. With daily reflection, you will check on your own activities, evaluate the progress, and make adjustments to ensure forward movement.

To make room and move toward the right actions, we need to consciously be aware of what we are doing, think about alternative choices, and analyze the benefits (rewards) of each choice. Spending a few minutes to reflect can change our entire path. When we spend time reflecting, we also notice progress, no matter how small it may seem. It is motivating to look back to see how far we've come. Reflecting helps us focus on the healthy strides, leading to more healthy strides.

Ultimately, daily reflection is the first step to learning from our experiences: what works and what does not, and what will move us toward achieving our goals and desires.

The Power of Gratitude:

Gratitude changes everything. — Anonymous

Gratitude is a virtue in every culture going back centuries. Cicero called gratitude "the parent of all other virtues." It's a pillar of all major religions, and almost everyone has come in contact with the concept in some way, shape, or form, whether on the news, in social media, or in topics of conversation. It makes sense that we would all be practicing gratitude because, in the many ways mentioned above, we have learned to appreciate it since childhood at home, in school, or through our spiritual practices.

While we intuitively know being grateful is a good thing, researchers have known for years that the practice of gratitude scientifically bolsters health and well-being, strengthens relationships, heightens success, creativity, self-esteem, and so much more.[4,5,6] Gratitude does this because each time we express sincere gratitude, we activate the brain's reward circuitry.

"How?" You may ask.

As we reflect on what we are thankful for, the hypothalamus is signaled to produce dopamine and serotonin - our brain's happy chemicals. These neurotransmitters fill us with pleasure, joy, and an enhanced sense of well-being. By making gratitude a daily practice, we stimulate new neural connections associated with joyful emotions. Neural pathways of thankfulness are strengthened in the brain through consistent use, creating automatic habits. With its plasticity, our brain structurally changes to find silver linings and blessings amid challenges readily. A mindset of gratitude allows us to see the good more easily, transforming how we experience life's journey. When we train our brain to focus on what it is grateful for, perspectives and the world around us shifts for the better.

Above is also why it's been proven over and over that grateful people have wider networks, enjoy greater support from more people, and are more socially secure.

Ironically, as we get older or as life's challenges begin, we can lose sight of it or take the practice for granted. Whether we practice it less and less or go in the direction of being ungrateful, it is easy to become consumed in fear, frustration, sadness, and anger and lose sight of how gratitude makes us feel.

It is in these times of struggle or doubt that consciously embracing gratitude is especially powerful. Giving thanks creates an uplifting environment that ripples outwards, inspiring those around us. Even when solutions seem scarce, gratitude fuels creativity and possibility thinking. It opens our eyes to silver linings we may have overlooked before. The consistent practice of seeking good actively trains the brain to find more blessings, big and small. As we focus on what brings joy and meaning, the more we express it, the more we see it multiplied in our lives. It fills us with hope and happiness from the inside out.

Forming a Healthy Habit:

"We are what we repeatedly do. Excellence, then, is not an act, but a habit." – Aristotle.

Forming a healthy habit or skill can take anywhere from 18 to 254 days, with 66 days being the average[8], and the only way to develop these new habits or skills is through constant & consistent repetition. Our journal provides the framework to achieve this through an initial 30-day Challenge leading to the remaining seventy days' worth of worksheets.

This journal embraces simplicity and repetition with intention. The power comes from your consistent engagement. Daily reflection and gratitude practices work best when kept straightforward to form lasting habits.

The brain thrives on repetition, and it takes consistent practice to reinforce neural pathways that uplift you. Even if uncomfortable or unnatural at first, keep feeding your mind through these daily practices.

Use this space to focus inward on your wellbeing and outward on your connections. Set and reflect on goals, give thanks, and take small actions to care for yourself. This practice has ripple effects - strengthening relationships and bringing more joy into each day.

We all need reminders to prioritize self-care. Give yourself permission to devote time to your mental, physical, and emotional health. This journey has the power to uplift you and those around you. With daily attention, you will build resilience from the inside out.

Before You Start

The only person you are destined to become is the person you decide to be. - Ralph Waldo Emerson

On the following few pages, you will need to jot down a brief snapshot about yourself; your bio/elevator pitch. If you do not have one handy, you can create one quickly. The elevator pitch describes who you are to the world, what you stand for, and what you do/want to do. This bio portrays how you want those around you to view and know you. How you see yourself and present yourself to the world are vital skills that we can all use practice honing. We are asking you to do this as a way to keep track of who you are, your wants and desires, as it is easy to lose oneself when faced with the various roles we all step into throughout the day.

When your elevator pitch is complete, you'll move on to create a Vision Board that highlights the goals and objectives you want to reach. It's one thing to have a elevator pitch, though in order to see the broader picture of your life and continue to move forward in your loved ones' recovery, it is essential to lay out what you want.

Each day, you'll reflect on whether your actions are aligned with what you want. This practice gives you the ability to stay hyper-focused on what you want and allows you to push through and achieve the goals you set quickly.

Want to super charge your practice and join a community of like-minded women? Scan our QR Code for instant access to free online lessons and join a community to rally behind and with!

I have
so
much to offer the
world.

Who I Am

*(Who am I? What do I enjoy? What have I achieved? What do I want to achieve? Who and what is important to me?
Include both professional and personal skills/goals/traits.)*

My Vision Board

Vision boards are a collage of images and words representing a person's wishes or goals. They inspire & motivate us to work towards what we want.
(I will write, draw, or attach pictures and words that reflect my goals.)

My Vision Board Continued

Starting Your Daily Challenge

Now that you've laid out your "bio/elevator pitch", and your visions and desires. It's time to start!

For the next 30 days, you will set aside 5 minutes first thing each morning (maybe with your coffee or tea in hand) for the first page and then again for 5 minutes at the end of the day for the second page. Try not to check your smartphone, read the news or emails, or succumb to other distractions around you.

You will focus on reflecting on the day before and acknowledge where you are and where you want to go by answering the daily questions listed in the workbook for each day. This is a place to keep track of your progress, achievements, joy, and where you are on this journey.

Be as specific with your gratitude and goals as possible, and be sure to feel them. Saying it is the start; knowing the whys and feeling them will propel you further.

When we start "thanking" what we have and leading with empathy and service, it opens the door for more of that in return for you.

Let's go!

I am COMMITTED to my self-care and well-being.

Day 1

How many hours of sleep did I get last night? _____

Today I'm feeling: *(Circle What Resonates)*

Exhausted   A bit tired   Refreshed   Like I can climb a mountain

Overall, I'm feeling:

Excited   Joyful   Okay   Overwhelmed   Down   _____

What can I do for me to keep or boost this mood?
(going for a 10-minute walk, catching up w/a friend, taking a class I love, tips in the back, etc)

_____

Today, I am grateful and happy for:
(start with one if you can't think of 3, the important part is to be specific and feel them)

1. _____
2. _____
3. _____

My desires and goals for today:

_____
_____
_____
_____
_____
_____
_____
_____

Today is: __ / __ / __

Today's challenges and/or what I am most proud of:

_____
_____
_____
_____
_____
_____

Who/what brought me joy, helped, or made me smile? _____

_____

Who did I show gratitude to today, and why? _____

_____

Tomorrow's Top Three Goals:

_____
_____
_____

Additional Thoughts:

_____
_____
_____
_____
_____

Day 2

How many hours of sleep did I get last night? _____

Today I'm feeling: *(Circle What Resonates)*

Exhausted   A bit tired   Refreshed   Like I can climb a mountain

Overall, I'm feeling:

Excited   Joyful   Okay   Overwhelmed   Down   _____

What can I do for me to keep or boost this mood?
(going for a 10-minute walk, catching up w/a friend, taking a class I love, tips in the back, etc)

_____

Today, I am grateful and happy for:
(start with one if you can't think of 3, the important part is to be specific and feel them)

1. _____
2. _____
3. _____

My desires and goals for today:

_____
_____
_____
_____
_____
_____
_____
_____

Today is: __/__/__

Today's challenges and/or what I am most proud of:

_____
_____
_____
_____
_____
_____

Who/what brought me joy, helped, or made me smile? _____

_____

Who did I show gratitude to today, and why? _____

_____

Tomorrow's Top Three Goals:

_____
_____
_____

Additional Thoughts:

_____
_____
_____
_____
_____

Day 3

How many hours of sleep did I get last night? _____

Today I'm feeling: *(Circle What Resonates)*

Exhausted   A bit tired   Refreshed   Like I can climb a mountain

Overall, I'm feeling:

Excited   Joyful   Okay   Overwhelmed   Down   _____

What can I do for me to keep or boost this mood?
(going for a 10-minute walk, catching up w/a friend, taking a class I love, tips in the back, etc)

_____

Today, I am grateful and happy for:
(start with one if you can't think of 3, the important part is to be specific and feel them)

1. _____
2. _____
3. _____

My desires and goals for today:

_____
_____
_____
_____
_____
_____
_____

Today is: __/__/__

Today's challenges and/or what I am most proud of:

_____

_____

_____

_____

_____

_____

Who/what brought me joy, helped, or made me smile? _____

_____

Who did I show gratitude to today, and why? _____

_____

Tomorrow's Top Three Goals:

_____

_____

_____

Additional Thoughts:

_____

_____

_____

_____

Day 4

How many hours of sleep did I get last night? _____

Today I'm feeling: (Circle What Resonates)

Exhausted   A bit tired   Refreshed   Like I can climb a mountain

Overall, I'm feeling:

Excited   Joyful   Okay   Overwhelmed   Down   _____

What can I do for me to keep or boost this mood?
(going for a 10-minute walk, catching up w/a friend, taking a class I love, tips in the back, etc)

_____

Today, I am grateful and happy for:
(start with one if you can't think of 3, the important part is to be specific and feel them)

1. _____
2. _____
3. _____

My desires and goals for today:

_____
_____
_____
_____
_____
_____
_____
_____

Today is: ___ / ___ / ___

Today's challenges and/or what I am most proud of:

_____
_____
_____
_____
_____
_____

Who/what brought me joy, helped, or made me smile? _____

_____

Who did I show gratitude to today, and why? _____

_____

Tomorrow's Top Three Goals:

_____
_____
_____

Additional Thoughts:

_____
_____
_____
_____

Day 5

How many hours of sleep did I get last night? _____

Today I'm feeling: *(Circle What Resonates)*

Exhausted   A bit tired   Refreshed   Like I can climb a mountain

Overall, I'm feeling:

Excited   Joyful   Okay   Overwhelmed   Down   _____

What can I do for me to keep or boost this mood?
(going for a 10-minute walk, catching up w/a friend, taking a class I love, tips in the back, etc)

_____

Today, I am grateful and happy for:
(start with one if you can't think of 3, the important part is to be specific and feel them)

1. _____
2. _____
3. _____

My desires and goals for today:

_____
_____
_____
_____
_____
_____
_____
_____

Today is: __ / __ / __

Today's challenges and/or what I am most proud of:

_____
_____
_____
_____
_____
_____

Who/what brought me joy, helped, or made me smile? _____

_____

Who did I show gratitude to today, and why? _____

_____

Tomorrow's Top Three Goals:

_____
_____
_____

Additional Thoughts:

_____
_____
_____
_____
_____

Day 6

How many hours of sleep did I get last night? _____

Today I'm feeling: *(Circle What Resonates)*

Exhausted   A bit tired   Refreshed   Like I can climb a mountain

Overall, I'm feeling:

Excited   Joyful   Okay   Overwhelmed   Down   _____

What can I do for me to keep or boost this mood?
(going for a 10-minute walk, catching up w/a friend, taking a class I love, tips in the back, etc)

_____

Today, I am grateful and happy for:
(start with one if you can't think of 3, the important part is to be specific and feel them)

1. _____
2. _____
3. _____

My desires and goals for today:

_____
_____
_____
_____
_____
_____
_____

Today is: __/__/__

Today's challenges and/or what I am most proud of:

_____
_____
_____
_____
_____
_____

Who/what brought me joy, helped, or made me smile? _____

_____

Who did I show gratitude to today, and why? _____

_____

Tomorrow's Top Three Goals:

_____
_____
_____

Additional Thoughts:

_____
_____
_____
_____

Day 7

How many hours of sleep did I get last night? _____

Today I'm feeling: *(Circle What Resonates)*

Exhausted   A bit tired   Refreshed   Like I can climb a mountain

Overall, I'm feeling:

Excited   Joyful   Okay   Overwhelmed   Down   _____

What can I do for me to keep or boost this mood?
(going for a 10-minute walk, catching up w/a friend, taking a class I love, tips in the back, etc)

_____

Today, I am grateful and happy for:
(start with one if you can't think of 3, the important part is to be specific and feel them)

1. _____
2. _____
3. _____

My desires and goals for today:

_____
_____
_____
_____
_____
_____
_____
_____

Today is: __ / __ / __

Today's challenges and/or what I am most proud of:

_____
_____
_____
_____
_____
_____

Who/what brought me joy, helped, or made me smile? _____

_____

Who did I show gratitude to today, and why? _____

_____

Tomorrow's Top Three Goals:

_____
_____
_____

Additional Thoughts:

_____
_____
_____
_____

Week One

Congrats, you finished week one of your 30 Day Gratitude Challenge!

*Reflect on this past week and then answer the following:
How do I feel? What have I learned? What did I accomplish? What feelings and habits do I want to keep? What excites me? What do I want to try or continue? Be descriptive.*

I forgive myself for any mistakes and I move FORWARD.

Day 8

How many hours of sleep did I get last night? _____

Today I'm feeling: *(Circle What Resonates)*

Exhausted   A bit tired   Refreshed   Like I can climb a mountain

Overall, I'm feeling:

Excited   Joyful   Okay   Overwhelmed   Down   _____

What can I do for me to keep or boost this mood?
(going for a 10-minute walk, catching up w/a friend, taking a class I love, tips in the back, etc)

Today, I am grateful and happy for:
(start with one if you can't think of 3, the important part is to be specific and feel them)

1. _____
2. _____
3. _____

My desires and goals for today:

_____
_____
_____
_____
_____
_____
_____

Today is: __ / __ / __

Today's challenges and/or what I am most proud of:

_____
_____
_____
_____
_____
_____

Who/what brought me joy, helped, or made me smile? _____

_____

Who did I show gratitude to today, and why? _____

_____

Tomorrow's Top Three Goals:

_____
_____
_____

Additional Thoughts:

_____
_____
_____
_____

Day 9

How many hours of sleep did I get last night? _____

Today I'm feeling: *(Circle What Resonates)*

Exhausted   A bit tired   Refreshed   Like I can climb a mountain

Overall, I'm feeling:

Excited   Joyful   Okay   Overwhelmed   Down   _____

What can I do for me to keep or boost this mood?
(going for a 10-minute walk, catching up w/a friend, taking a class I love, tips in the back, etc)

Today, I am grateful and happy for:
(start with one if you can't think of 3, the important part is to be specific and feel them)

1. _____
2. _____
3. _____

My desires and goals for today:

_____
_____
_____
_____
_____
_____
_____

Today is: __ / __ / __

Today's challenges and/or what I am most proud of:

_____
_____
_____
_____
_____

Who/what brought me joy, helped, or made me smile? _____

_____

Who did I show gratitude to today, and why? _____

_____

Tomorrow's Top Three Goals:

_____
_____
_____

Additional Thoughts:

_____
_____
_____
_____

Day 10

How many hours of sleep did I get last night? _____

Today I'm feeling:

Exhausted   A bit tired   Refreshed   Like I can climb a mountain

Overall, I'm feeling:

Excited   Joyful   Okay   Overwhelmed   Down   _____

What will I do for me to keep or boost this mood?

_____

Today, I am grateful and happy for:

1. _____
2. _____
3. _____

My desires and goals for today:

_____

_____

_____

_____

_____

_____

_____

Today is: __ / __ / __

Today's challenges and/or what I am most proud of:

_____
_____
_____
_____
_____
_____

Who/what brought me joy, helped, or made me smile? _____

_____

Who did I show gratitude to today, and why? _____

_____

Tomorrow's Top Three Goals:

_____
_____
_____

Additional Thoughts:

_____
_____
_____
_____

Day 11

How many hours of sleep did I get last night? _____

Today I'm feeling:

Exhausted   A bit tired   Refreshed   Like I can climb a mountain

Overall, I'm feeling:

Excited   Joyful   Okay   Overwhelmed   Down   _____

What will I do for me to keep or boost this mood?

_____

Today, I am grateful and happy for:

1. _____
2. _____
3. _____

My desires and goals for today:

_____
_____
_____
_____
_____
_____
_____

Today is: ___ / ___ / ___

Today's challenges and/or what I am most proud of:

_____

_____

_____

_____

_____

_____

Who/what brought me joy, helped, or made me smile? _____

_____

Who did I show gratitude to today, and why? _____

_____

Tomorrow's Top Three Goals:

_____

_____

_____

Additional Thoughts:

_____

_____

_____

_____

_____

Day 12

How many hours of sleep did I get last night? _____

Today I'm feeling:

   Exhausted   A bit tired   Refreshed   Like I can climb a mountain

Overall, I'm feeling:

Excited   Joyful   Okay   Overwhelmed   Down   _____

What will I do for me to keep or boost this mood?

_____

Today, I am grateful and happy for:

1. _____
2. _____
3. _____

My desires and goals for today:

_____
_____
_____
_____
_____
_____
_____
_____

Today is: __ / __ / __

Today's challenges and/or what I am most proud of:

_____
_____
_____
_____
_____
_____

Who/what brought me joy, helped, or made me smile? _____

_____

Who did I show gratitude to today, and why? _____

_____

Tomorrow's Top Three Goals:

_____
_____
_____

Additional Thoughts:

_____
_____
_____
_____
_____

Day 13

How many hours of sleep did I get last night? _____

Today I'm feeling:

Exhausted   A bit tired   Refreshed   Like I can climb a mountain

Overall, I'm feeling:

Excited   Joyful   Okay   Overwhelmed   Down   _____

What will I do for me to keep or boost this mood?

_____

Today, I am grateful and happy for:

1. _____
2. _____
3. _____

My desires and goals for today:

_____
_____
_____
_____
_____
_____
_____

Today is: __ / __ / __

Today's challenges and/or what I am most proud of:

_____
_____
_____
_____
_____
_____

Who/what brought me joy, helped, or made me smile? _____

_____

Who did I show gratitude to today, and why? _____

_____

Tomorrow's Top Three Goals:

_____
_____
_____

Additional Thoughts:

_____
_____
_____
_____
_____

Day 14

How many hours of sleep did I get last night? _____

Today I'm feeling:

Exhausted   A bit tired   Refreshed   Like I can climb a mountain

Overall, I'm feeling:

Excited   Joyful   Okay   Overwhelmed   Down   _____

What will I do for me to keep or boost this mood?

_____

Today, I am grateful and happy for:

1. _____
2. _____
3. _____

My desires and goals for today:

_____
_____
_____
_____
_____
_____
_____

Today is: __ / __ / __

Today's challenges and/or what I am most proud of:

_____
_____
_____
_____
_____
_____

Who/what brought me joy, helped, or made me smile? _____

_____

Who did I show gratitude to today, and why? _____

_____

Tomorrow's Top Three Goals:

_____
_____
_____

Additional Thoughts:

_____
_____
_____
_____
_____

Week Two

You're halfway there, two more weeks to go.

*Reflect on this past week and then answer the following:
How do I feel? What have I learned? What did I accomplish? What good has happened? What do I want to try or continue? Be descriptive.*

I nurture my spirit through activities I enjoy.

Day 15

How many hours of sleep did I get last night? _____

Today I'm feeling:

Exhausted   A bit tired   Refreshed   Like I can climb a mountain

Overall, I'm feeling:

Excited   Joyful   Okay   Overwhelmed   Down   _____

What will I do for me to keep or boost this mood?

_____

Today, I am grateful and happy for:

1. _____
2. _____
3. _____

My desires and goals for today:

_____
_____
_____
_____
_____
_____
_____

Today is: __ / __ / __

Today's challenges and/or what I am most proud of:

_____
_____
_____
_____
_____
_____

Who/what brought me joy, helped, or made me smile? _____

_____

Who did I show gratitude to today, and why? _____

_____

Tomorrow's Top Three Goals:

_____
_____
_____

Additional Thoughts:

_____
_____
_____
_____

Day 16

How many hours of sleep did I get last night? _____

Today I'm feeling:

Exhausted   A bit tired   Refreshed   Like I can climb a mountain

Overall, I'm feeling:

Excited   Joyful   Okay   Overwhelmed   Down   _____

What will I do for me to keep or boost this mood?

_____

Today, I am grateful and happy for:

1. _____
2. _____
3. _____

My desires and goals for today:

_____
_____
_____
_____
_____
_____
_____

Today is: __ / __ / __

Today's challenges and/or what I am most proud of:

_____
_____
_____
_____
_____

Who/what brought me joy, helped, or made me smile? _____

_____

Who did I show gratitude to today, and why? _____

_____

Tomorrow's Top Three Goals:

_____
_____
_____

Additional Thoughts:

_____
_____
_____
_____
_____

Day 17

How many hours of sleep did I get last night? _____

Today I'm feeling:

Exhausted   A bit tired   Refreshed   Like I can climb a mountain

Overall, I'm feeling:

Excited   Joyful   Okay   Overwhelmed   Down   _____

What will I do for me to keep or boost this mood?

_____

Today, I am grateful and happy for:

1. _____
2. _____
3. _____

My desires and goals for today:

_____
_____
_____
_____
_____
_____
_____

Today is: __ / __ / __

Today's challenges and/or what I am most proud of:

_____
_____
_____
_____
_____
_____

Who/what brought me joy, helped, or made me smile? _____

_____

Who did I show gratitude to today, and why? _____

_____

Tomorrow's Top Three Goals:

_____
_____
_____

Additional Thoughts:

_____
_____
_____
_____

Day 18

How many hours of sleep did I get last night? _____

Today I'm feeling:

Exhausted   A bit tired   Refreshed   Like I can climb a mountain

Overall, I'm feeling:

Excited   Joyful   Okay   Overwhelmed   Down   _____

What will I do for me to keep or boost this mood?

_____

Today, I am grateful and happy for:

1. _____
2. _____
3. _____

My desires and goals for today:

_____
_____
_____
_____
_____
_____
_____

Today is: __ / __ / __

Today's challenges and/or what I am most proud of:

_____
_____
_____
_____
_____
_____

Who/what brought me joy, helped, or made me smile? _____

_____

Who did I show gratitude to today, and why? _____

_____

Tomorrow's Top Three Goals:

_____
_____
_____

Additional Thoughts:

_____
_____
_____
_____
_____

Day 19

How many hours of sleep did I get last night? _____

Today I'm feeling:

Exhausted   A bit tired   Refreshed   Like I can climb a mountain

Overall, I'm feeling:

Excited   Joyful   Okay   Overwhelmed   Down   _____

What will I do for me to keep or boost this mood?

_____

Today, I am grateful and happy for:

1. _____
2. _____
3. _____

My desires and goals for today:

_____
_____
_____
_____
_____
_____
_____

Today is: __ / __ / __

Today's challenges and/or what I am most proud of:

_____
_____
_____
_____
_____
_____

Who/what brought me joy, helped, or made me smile? _____

_____

Who did I show gratitude to today, and why? _____

_____

Tomorrow's Top Three Goals:

_____
_____
_____

Additional Thoughts:

_____
_____
_____
_____
_____

Day 20

How many hours of sleep did I get last night? _____

Today I'm feeling:

Exhausted   A bit tired   Refreshed   Like I can climb a mountain

Overall, I'm feeling:

Excited   Joyful   Okay   Overwhelmed   Down   _____

What will I do for me to keep or boost this mood?

_____

Today, I am grateful and happy for:

1. _____
2. _____
3. _____

My desires and goals for today:

_____
_____
_____
_____
_____
_____
_____

Today is: __ / __ / __

Today's challenges and/or what I am most proud of:

_____
_____
_____
_____
_____
_____

Who/what brought me joy, helped, or made me smile? _____

_____

Who did I show gratitude to today, and why? _____

_____

Tomorrow's Top Three Goals:

_____
_____
_____

Additional Thoughts:

_____
_____
_____
_____

Day 21

How many hours of sleep did I get last night? _____

Today I'm feeling:

Exhausted   A bit tired   Refreshed   Like I can climb a mountain

Overall, I'm feeling:

Excited   Joyful   Okay   Overwhelmed   Down   _____

What will I do for me to keep or boost this mood?

_____

Today, I am grateful and happy for:

1. _____
2. _____
3. _____

My desires and goals for today:

_____
_____
_____
_____
_____
_____
_____

Today is: __ / __ / __

Today's challenges and/or what I am most proud of:

_____
_____
_____
_____
_____
_____

Who/what brought me joy, helped, or made me smile? _____

_____

Who did I show gratitude to today, and why? _____

_____

Tomorrow's Top Three Goals:

_____
_____
_____

Additional Thoughts:

_____
_____
_____
_____
_____

Week Three

You're almost free.

*Reflect on this past week and then answer the following:
How do I feel? What have I learned? What did I accomplish? What good
has happened? What do I want to try or continue? Be descriptive.*

Doing my best is always ENOUGH.

Day 22

How many hours of sleep did I get last night? _____

Today I'm feeling:

Exhausted   A bit tired   Refreshed   Like I can climb a mountain

Overall, I'm feeling:

Excited   Joyful   Okay   Overwhelmed   Down   _____

What will I do for me to keep or boost this mood?

_____

Today, I am grateful and happy for:

1. _____
2. _____
3. _____

My desires and goals for today:

_____
_____
_____
_____
_____
_____
_____
_____

Today is: __ / __ / __

Today's challenges and/or what I am most proud of:

_____
_____
_____
_____
_____
_____

Who/what brought me joy, helped, or made me smile? _____

_____

Who did I show gratitude to today, and why? _____

_____

Tomorrow's Top Three Goals:

_____
_____
_____

Additional Thoughts:

_____
_____
_____
_____

Day 23

How many hours of sleep did I get last night? _____

Today I'm feeling:

Exhausted   A bit tired   Refreshed   Like I can climb a mountain

Overall, I'm feeling:

Excited   Joyful   Okay   Overwhelmed   Down   _____

What will I do for me to keep or boost this mood?

_____

Today, I am grateful and happy for:

1. _____
2. _____
3. _____

My desires and goals for today:

_____
_____
_____
_____
_____
_____
_____
_____

Today is: __ / __ / __

Today's challenges and/or what I am most proud of:

_____
_____
_____
_____
_____
_____

Who/what brought me joy, helped, or made me smile? _____

_____

Who did I show gratitude to today, and why? _____

_____

Tomorrow's Top Three Goals:

_____
_____
_____

Additional Thoughts:

_____
_____
_____
_____
_____

Day 24

How many hours of sleep did I get last night? _____

Today I'm feeling:

Exhausted   A bit tired   Refreshed   Like I can climb a mountain

Overall, I'm feeling:

Excited   Joyful   Okay   Overwhelmed   Down   _____

What will I do for me to keep or boost this mood?

_____

Today, I am grateful and happy for:

1. _____
2. _____
3. _____

My desires and goals for today:

_____
_____
_____
_____
_____
_____
_____
_____

Today is: __ / __ / __

Today's challenges and/or what I am most proud of:

_____
_____
_____
_____
_____
_____

Who/what brought me joy, helped, or made me smile? _____

_____

Who did I show gratitude to today, and why? _____

_____

Tomorrow's Top Three Goals:

_____
_____
_____

Additional Thoughts:

_____
_____
_____
_____
_____

Day 25

How many hours of sleep did I get last night? _____

Today I'm feeling:

Exhausted   A bit tired   Refreshed   Like I can climb a mountain

Overall, I'm feeling:

Excited   Joyful   Okay   Overwhelmed   Down   _____

What will I do for me to keep or boost this mood?

_____

Today, I am grateful and happy for:

1. _____
2. _____
3. _____

My desires and goals for today:

_____
_____
_____
_____
_____
_____
_____
_____

Today is: __ / __ / __

Today's challenges and/or what I am most proud of:

_____
_____
_____
_____
_____
_____

Who/what brought me joy, helped, or made me smile? _____

_____

Who did I show gratitude to today, and why? _____

_____

Tomorrow's Top Three Goals:

_____
_____
_____

Additional Thoughts:

_____
_____
_____
_____

Day 26

How many hours of sleep did I get last night? _____

Today I'm feeling:

Exhausted   A bit tired   Refreshed   Like I can climb a mountain

Overall, I'm feeling:

Excited   Joyful   Okay   Overwhelmed   Down   _____

What will I do for me to keep or boost this mood?

_____

Today, I am grateful and happy for:

1. _____
2. _____
3. _____

My desires and goals for today:

_____

_____

_____

_____

_____

_____

_____

Today is: __ / __ / __

Today's challenges and/or what I am most proud of:

_____
_____
_____
_____
_____
_____

Who/what brought me joy, helped, or made me smile? _____

_____

Who did I show gratitude to today, and why? _____

_____

Tomorrow's Top Three Goals:

_____
_____
_____

Additional Thoughts:

_____
_____
_____
_____
_____

Day 27

How many hours of sleep did I get last night? _____

Today I'm feeling:

Exhausted   A bit tired   Refreshed   Like I can climb a mountain

Overall, I'm feeling:

Excited   Joyful   Okay   Overwhelmed   Down   _____

What will I do for me to keep or boost this mood?

_____

Today, I am grateful and happy for:

1. _____
2. _____
3. _____

My desires and goals for today:

_____
_____
_____
_____
_____
_____
_____

Today is: __ / __ / __

Today's challenges and/or what I am most proud of:

_____
_____
_____
_____
_____
_____

Who/what brought me joy, helped, or made me smile? _____

_____

Who did I show gratitude to today, and why? _____

_____

Tomorrow's Top Three Goals:

_____
_____
_____

Additional Thoughts:

_____
_____
_____
_____
_____

Day 28

How many hours of sleep did I get last night? _____

Today I'm feeling:

Exhausted   A bit tired   Refreshed   Like I can climb a mountain

Overall, I'm feeling:

Excited   Joyful   Okay   Overwhelmed   Down   _____

What will I do for me to keep or boost this mood?

_____

Today, I am grateful and happy for:

1. _____
2. _____
3. _____

My desires and goals for today:

_____
_____
_____
_____
_____
_____
_____
_____

Today is: ___ / ___ / ___

Today's challenges and/or what I am most proud of:

_____
_____
_____
_____
_____
_____

Who/what brought me joy, helped, or made me smile? _____

_____

Who did I show gratitude to today, and why? _____

_____

Tomorrow's Top Three Goals:

_____
_____
_____

Additional Thoughts:

_____
_____
_____
_____

Week Four

Two More Days to Go.

*Reflect on this past week and then answer the following:
How do I feel? What have I learned? What did I accomplish? What good has happened? What do I want to try or continue? Be descriptive.*

It's okay to ask for help; seeking support is a sign of STRENGTH.

Day 29

How many hours of sleep did I get last night? _____

Today I'm feeling:

Exhausted   A bit tired   Refreshed   Like I can climb a mountain

Overall, I'm feeling:

Excited   Joyful   Okay   Overwhelmed   Down   _____

What will I do for me to keep or boost this mood?
_____

Today, I am grateful and happy for:

1. _____
2. _____
3. _____

My desires and goals for today:

_____
_____
_____
_____
_____
_____
_____

Today is: __ / __ / __

Today's challenges and/or what I am most proud of:

_____
_____
_____
_____
_____
_____

Who/what brought me joy, helped, or made me smile? _____
_____

Who did I show gratitude to today, and why? _____
_____

Tomorrow's Top Three Goals:

_____
_____
_____

Additional Thoughts:

_____
_____
_____
_____
_____

Day 30

How many hours of sleep did I get last night? _____

Today I'm feeling:

Exhausted   A bit tired   Refreshed   Like I can climb a mountain

Overall, I'm feeling:

Excited   Joyful   Okay   Overwhelmed   Down   _____

What will I do for me to keep or boost this mood?

_____

Today, I am grateful and happy for:

1. _____
2. _____
3. _____

My desires and goals for today:

_____
_____
_____
_____
_____
_____
_____

Today is: __ / __ / __

Today's challenges and/or what I am most proud of:

_____
_____
_____
_____
_____
_____

Who/what brought me joy, helped, or made me smile? _____

_____

Who did I show gratitude to today, and why? _____

_____

Tomorrow's Top Three Goals:

_____
_____
_____

Additional Thoughts:

_____
_____
_____
_____

I choose thoughts that make me feel empowered and uplifted

You Did It!!

30 Days! An accomplishment you should be proud of.

You know the drill. Reflect on this past month and answer the following: How do I feel? What have I learned? What did I accomplish? What good has happened? What do I want to try or continue? Be descriptive.

Notes, Thoughts, Reflections

(This space is for additional thoughts or feelings I may have, remembering to also keep them focused on items I want to happen or do.)

Notes, Thoughts, Reflections

My Vision Board

*Looking back at my vision board at the start of this challenge...
Did it stay the same? Did it change?
(If it changed, this space is to create an updated vision board. If it stayed the same,
I can recreate it here to make my vision even stronger.)*

My Vision Board Continued

I practice gratitude for all the BLESSINGS in my life.

Conclusion

We are all here to find our paths and joy. We are, and you should be proud of your efforts to care for yourself. It is vital to prioritize self-care, not only for yourself but also for your loved ones and those around you.

We hope you have come to see how Reflection and Gratitude can help you to keep moving forward when things feel impossible, that is has allowed you to see just how far you've come, and that it has provided the dopamine and serotonin needed for joy, solution-finding, health, creativity, and so much more.

We hope the past 30 days and this journal have helped you create a new morning and evening ritual that brings you joy, learning, and a greater appreciation for yourself and those around you.

While it can take anywhere from 18 to 254 days (66 on average) to form a new habit, you are well on your way to having all of this stick if they haven't already.

Our goal was to provide you with the framework to practice reflection and Gratitude daily and show you that a little can go a long way in your current journey. If we've succeeded, we'd love to hear from you at hello@hamptonsbossmoms.com.

Now what? Keep up the excellent work! We've included an additional 70 Days to round out 100 days of Gratitude and set you up for the next 100 days, should you want to keep going.

Exploring Paths Publishing also supports workbooks for all ages and in multiple languages, so take your learnings home and share a 30-Day Challenge with your family or friends.

For more information and further resources, please visit exploringpathspublishing.com

> With Gratitude, We're cheering you on!
> Katherine & Kim

I find small JOYS and GRATITUDES in my everyday experiences.

Bonus!

Day 31

How many hours of sleep did I get last night? _____

Today I'm feeling:

Exhausted   A bit tired   Refreshed   Like I can climb a mountain

Overall, I'm feeling:

Excited   Joyful   Okay   Overwhelmed   Down   _____

What will I do for me to keep or boost this mood?

_____

Today, I am grateful and happy for:

1. _____
2. _____
3. _____

My desires and goals for today:

_____
_____
_____
_____
_____
_____
_____

Today is: __ / __ / __

Today's challenges and/or what I am most proud of:

_____
_____
_____
_____
_____
_____

Who/what brought me joy, helped, or made me smile? _____

_____

Who did I show gratitude to today, and why? _____

_____

Tomorrow's Top Three Goals:

_____
_____
_____

Additional Thoughts:

_____
_____
_____
_____
_____

Day 32

How many hours of sleep did I get last night? _____

Today I'm feeling:

Exhausted   A bit tired   Refreshed   Like I can climb a mountain

Overall, I'm feeling:

Excited   Joyful   Okay   Overwhelmed   Down   _____

What will I do for me to keep or boost this mood?

_____

Today, I am grateful and happy for:

1. _____
2. _____
3. _____

My desires and goals for today:

_____
_____
_____
_____
_____
_____
_____

Today is: __/__/__

Today's challenges and/or what I am most proud of:

_____
_____
_____
_____
_____
_____

Who/what brought me joy, helped, or made me smile? _____

_____

Who did I show gratitude to today, and why? _____

_____

Tomorrow's Top Three Goals:

_____
_____
_____

Additional Thoughts:

_____
_____
_____
_____

Day 33

How many hours of sleep did I get last night? _____

Today I'm feeling:

Exhausted   A bit tired   Refreshed   Like I can climb a mountain

Overall, I'm feeling:

Excited   Joyful   Okay   Overwhelmed   Down   _____

What will I do for me to keep or boost this mood?

_____

Today, I am grateful and happy for:

1. _____
2. _____
3. _____

My desires and goals for today:

_____
_____
_____
_____
_____
_____
_____

Today is: __ / __ / __

Today's challenges and/or what I am most proud of:

_____
_____
_____
_____
_____
_____

Who/what brought me joy, helped, or made me smile? _____

_____

Who did I show gratitude to today, and why? _____

_____

Tomorrow's Top Three Goals:

_____
_____
_____

Additional Thoughts:

_____
_____
_____
_____

Day 34

How many hours of sleep did I get last night? _____

Today I'm feeling:

Exhausted   A bit tired   Refreshed   Like I can climb a mountain

Overall, I'm feeling:

Excited   Joyful   Okay   Overwhelmed   Down   _____

What will I do for me to keep or boost this mood?

_____

Today, I am grateful and happy for:

1. _____
2. _____
3. _____

My desires and goals for today:

_____
_____
_____
_____
_____
_____
_____
_____

Today is: __ / __ / __

Today's challenges and/or what I am most proud of:

___

Who/what brought me joy, helped, or made me smile? ___

___

Who did I show gratitude to today, and why? ___

___

Tomorrow's Top Three Goals:

___

Additional Thoughts:

___

Day 35

How many hours of sleep did I get last night? _____

Today I'm feeling:

Exhausted   A bit tired   Refreshed   Like I can climb a mountain

Overall, I'm feeling:

Excited   Joyful   Okay   Overwhelmed   Down   _____

What will I do for me to keep or boost this mood?

_____

Today, I am grateful and happy for:

1. _____
2. _____
3. _____

My desires and goals for today:

_____
_____
_____
_____
_____
_____
_____

Today is: __ / __ / __

Today's challenges and/or what I am most proud of:

_____
_____
_____
_____
_____
_____

Who/what brought me joy, helped, or made me smile? _____

_____

Who did I show gratitude to today, and why? _____

_____

Tomorrow's Top Three Goals:

_____
_____
_____

Additional Thoughts:

_____
_____
_____
_____
_____

Day 36

How many hours of sleep did I get last night? _____

Today I'm feeling:

Exhausted   A bit tired   Refreshed   Like I can climb a mountain

Overall, I'm feeling:

Excited   Joyful   Okay   Overwhelmed   Down   _____

What will I do for me to keep or boost this mood?

_____

Today, I am grateful and happy for:

1. _____
2. _____
3. _____

My desires and goals for today:

_____
_____
_____
_____
_____
_____
_____
_____

Today is: __/__/__

Today's challenges and/or what I am most proud of:

_____
_____
_____
_____
_____
_____
_____

Who/what brought me joy, helped, or made me smile? _____

_____

Who did I show gratitude to today, and why? _____

_____

Tomorrow's Top Three Goals:

_____
_____
_____

Additional Thoughts:

_____
_____
_____
_____
_____

Day 37

How many hours of sleep did I get last night? _____

Today I'm feeling:

Exhausted   A bit tired   Refreshed   Like I can climb a mountain

Overall, I'm feeling:

Excited   Joyful   Okay   Overwhelmed   Down   _____

What will I do for me to keep or boost this mood?

_____

Today, I am grateful and happy for:

1. _____
2. _____
3. _____

My desires and goals for today:

_____
_____
_____
_____
_____
_____
_____
_____

Today is: __/__/__

Today's challenges and/or what I am most proud of:

_____
_____
_____
_____
_____
_____

Who/what brought me joy, helped, or made me smile? _____

_____

Who did I show gratitude to today, and why? _____

_____

Tomorrow's Top Three Goals:

_____
_____
_____

Additional Thoughts:

_____
_____
_____
_____
_____

Day 38

How many hours of sleep did I get last night? _____

Today I'm feeling:

Exhausted   A bit tired   Refreshed   Like I can climb a mountain

Overall, I'm feeling:

Excited   Joyful   Okay   Overwhelmed   Down   _____

What will I do for me to keep or boost this mood?

_____

Today, I am grateful and happy for:

1. _____
2. _____
3. _____

My desires and goals for today:

_____
_____
_____
_____
_____
_____
_____

Today is: __ / __ / __

Today's challenges and/or what I am most proud of:

_____
_____
_____
_____
_____
_____

Who/what brought me joy, helped, or made me smile? _____

_____

Who did I show gratitude to today, and why? _____

_____

Tomorrow's Top Three Goals:

_____
_____
_____

Additional Thoughts:

_____
_____
_____
_____
_____

Day 39

How many hours of sleep did I get last night? _____

Today I'm feeling:

Exhausted   A bit tired   Refreshed   Like I can climb a mountain

Overall, I'm feeling:

Excited   Joyful   Okay   Overwhelmed   Down   _____

What will I do for me to keep or boost this mood?

_____

Today, I am grateful and happy for:

1. _____
2. _____
3. _____

My desires and goals for today:

_____
_____
_____
_____
_____
_____
_____

Today is: __ / __ / __

Today's challenges and/or what I am most proud of:

_____

_____

_____

_____

_____

_____

Who/what brought me joy, helped, or made me smile? _____

_____

Who did I show gratitude to today, and why? _____

_____

Tomorrow's Top Three Goals:

_____

_____

_____

Additional Thoughts:

_____

_____

_____

_____

Day 40

How many hours of sleep did I get last night? _____

Today I'm feeling:

Exhausted   A bit tired   Refreshed   Like I can climb a mountain

Overall, I'm feeling:

Excited   Joyful   Okay   Overwhelmed   Down   _____

What will I do for me to keep or boost this mood?

_____

Today, I am grateful and happy for:

1. _____
2. _____
3. _____

My desires and goals for today:

_____
_____
_____
_____
_____
_____
_____
_____

Today is: __ / __ / __

Today's challenges and/or what I am most proud of:

_____
_____
_____
_____
_____
_____

Who/what brought me joy, helped, or made me smile? _____

_____

Who did I show gratitude to today, and why? _____

_____

Tomorrow's Top Three Goals:

_____
_____
_____

Additional Thoughts:

_____
_____
_____
_____
_____

Day 41

How many hours of sleep did I get last night? _____

Today I'm feeling:

Exhausted   A bit tired   Refreshed   Like I can climb a mountain

Overall, I'm feeling:

Excited   Joyful   Okay   Overwhelmed   Down   _____

What will I do for me to keep or boost this mood?

_____

Today, I am grateful and happy for:

1. _____
2. _____
3. _____

My desires and goals for today:

_____
_____
_____
_____
_____
_____
_____

Today is: ___ / ___ / ___

Today's challenges and/or what I am most proud of:

_____
_____
_____
_____
_____
_____

Who/what brought me joy, helped, or made me smile? _____

_____

Who did I show gratitude to today, and why? _____

_____

Tomorrow's Top Three Goals:

_____
_____
_____

Additional Thoughts:

_____
_____
_____
_____
_____

Day 42

How many hours of sleep did I get last night? _____

Today I'm feeling:

Exhausted   A bit tired   Refreshed   Like I can climb a mountain

Overall, I'm feeling:

Excited   Joyful   Okay   Overwhelmed   Down   _____

What will I do for me to keep or boost this mood?

_____

Today, I am grateful and happy for:

1. _____
2. _____
3. _____

My desires and goals for today:

_____
_____
_____
_____
_____
_____
_____

Today is: __ / __ / __

Today's challenges and/or what I am most proud of:

_____
_____
_____
_____
_____
_____

Who/what brought me joy, helped, or made me smile? _____

_____

Who did I show gratitude to today, and why? _____

_____

Tomorrow's Top Three Goals:

_____
_____
_____

Additional Thoughts:

_____
_____
_____
_____
_____

Day 43

How many hours of sleep did I get last night? _____

Today I'm feeling:

Exhausted   A bit tired   Refreshed   Like I can climb a mountain

Overall, I'm feeling:

Excited   Joyful   Okay   Overwhelmed   Down   _____

What will I do for me to keep or boost this mood?

_____

Today, I am grateful and happy for:

1. _____
2. _____
3. _____

My desires and goals for today:

_____
_____
_____
_____
_____
_____
_____

Today is: __ / __ / __

Today's challenges and/or what I am most proud of:

_____
_____
_____
_____
_____
_____

Who/what brought me joy, helped, or made me smile? _____

_____

Who did I show gratitude to today, and why? _____

_____

Tomorrow's Top Three Goals:

_____
_____
_____

Additional Thoughts:

_____
_____
_____
_____
_____

Day 44

How many hours of sleep did I get last night? _____

Today I'm feeling:

Exhausted   A bit tired   Refreshed   Like I can climb a mountain

Overall, I'm feeling:

Excited   Joyful   Okay   Overwhelmed   Down   _____

What will I do for me to keep or boost this mood?

_____

Today, I am grateful and happy for:

1. _____
2. _____
3. _____

My desires and goals for today:

_____

_____

_____

_____

_____

_____

_____

Today is: __ / __ / __

Today's challenges and/or what I am most proud of:

_____
_____
_____
_____
_____
_____

Who/what brought me joy, helped, or made me smile? _____

_____

Who did I show gratitude to today, and why? _____

_____

Tomorrow's Top Three Goals:

_____
_____
_____

Additional Thoughts:

_____
_____
_____
_____
_____

Day 45

How many hours of sleep did I get last night? _____

Today I'm feeling:

Exhausted   A bit tired   Refreshed   Like I can climb a mountain

Overall, I'm feeling:

Excited   Joyful   Okay   Overwhelmed   Down   _____

What will I do for me to keep or boost this mood?

_____

Today, I am grateful and happy for:

1. _____
2. _____
3. _____

My desires and goals for today:

_____
_____
_____
_____
_____
_____
_____

Today is: __ / __ / __

Today's challenges and/or what I am most proud of:

_____
_____
_____
_____
_____
_____

Who/what brought me joy, helped, or made me smile? _____

_____

Who did I show gratitude to today, and why? _____

_____

Tomorrow's Top Three Goals:

_____
_____
_____

Additional Thoughts:

_____
_____
_____
_____

Day 46

How many hours of sleep did I get last night? _____

Today I'm feeling:
Exhausted   A bit tired   Refreshed   Like I can climb a mountain

Overall, I'm feeling:
Excited   Joyful   Okay   Overwhelmed   Down   _____

What will I do for me to keep or boost this mood?
_____

Today, I am grateful and happy for:
1. _____
2. _____
3. _____

My desires and goals for today:
_____
_____
_____
_____
_____
_____
_____

Today is: __ / __ / __

Today's challenges and/or what I am most proud of:

_____
_____
_____
_____
_____
_____

Who/what brought me joy, helped, or made me smile? _____

_____

Who did I show gratitude to today, and why? _____

_____

Tomorrow's Top Three Goals:

_____
_____
_____

Additional Thoughts:

_____
_____
_____
_____
_____

Day 47

How many hours of sleep did I get last night? _____

Today I'm feeling:

Exhausted   A bit tired   Refreshed   Like I can climb a mountain

Overall, I'm feeling:

Excited   Joyful   Okay   Overwhelmed   Down   _____

What will I do for me to keep or boost this mood?

_____

Today, I am grateful and happy for:

1. _____
2. _____
3. _____

My desires and goals for today:

_____
_____
_____
_____
_____
_____
_____

Today is: __ / __ / __

Today's challenges and/or what I am most proud of:

_____
_____
_____
_____
_____
_____

Who/what brought me joy, helped, or made me smile? _____

_____

Who did I show gratitude to today, and why? _____

_____

Tomorrow's Top Three Goals:

_____
_____
_____

Additional Thoughts:

_____
_____
_____
_____
_____

Day 48

How many hours of sleep did I get last night? _____

Today I'm feeling:

Exhausted   A bit tired   Refreshed   Like I can climb a mountain

Overall, I'm feeling:

Excited   Joyful   Okay   Overwhelmed   Down   _____

What will I do for me to keep or boost this mood?

_____

Today, I am grateful and happy for:

1. _____
2. _____
3. _____

My desires and goals for today:

_____
_____
_____
_____
_____
_____
_____

Today is: __ / __ / __

Today's challenges and/or what I am most proud of:

Who/what brought me joy, helped, or made me smile? ———

Who did I show gratitude to today, and why? ———

Tomorrow's Top Three Goals:

Additional Thoughts:

Day 49

How many hours of sleep did I get last night? _____

Today I'm feeling:

Exhausted   A bit tired   Refreshed   Like I can climb a mountain

Overall, I'm feeling:

Excited   Joyful   Okay   Overwhelmed   Down   _____

What will I do for me to keep or boost this mood?

_____

Today, I am grateful and happy for:

1. _____
2. _____
3. _____

My desires and goals for today:

_____
_____
_____
_____
_____
_____
_____

Today is: __ / __ / __

Today's challenges and/or what I am most proud of:

_____
_____
_____
_____
_____
_____
_____

Who/what brought me joy, helped, or made me smile? _____

_____

Who did I show gratitude to today, and why? _____

_____

Tomorrow's Top Three Goals:

_____
_____
_____

Additional Thoughts:

_____
_____
_____
_____
_____

Day 50

How many hours of sleep did I get last night? _____

Today I'm feeling:

Exhausted   A bit tired   Refreshed   Like I can climb a mountain

Overall, I'm feeling:

Excited   Joyful   Okay   Overwhelmed   Down   _____

What will I do for me to keep or boost this mood?
_____

Today, I am grateful and happy for:

1. _____
2. _____
3. _____

My desires and goals for today:

_____
_____
_____
_____
_____
_____
_____

Today is: __/__/__

Today's challenges and/or what I am most proud of:

_____
_____
_____
_____
_____
_____

Who/what brought me joy, helped, or made me smile? _____

_____

Who did I show gratitude to today, and why? _____

_____

Tomorrow's Top Three Goals:

_____
_____
_____

Additional Thoughts:

_____
_____
_____
_____
_____

Day 51

How many hours of sleep did I get last night? _____

Today I'm feeling:

  Exhausted   A bit tired   Refreshed   Like I can climb a mountain

Overall, I'm feeling:

  Excited   Joyful   Okay   Overwhelmed   Down   _____

What will I do for me to keep or boost this mood?

_____

Today, I am grateful and happy for:

1. _____
2. _____
3. _____

My desires and goals for today:

_____
_____
_____
_____
_____
_____
_____
_____

Today is: __ / __ / __

Today's challenges and/or what I am most proud of:

_____
_____
_____
_____
_____
_____

Who/what brought me joy, helped, or made me smile? _____

_____

Who did I show gratitude to today, and why? _____

_____

Tomorrow's Top Three Goals:

_____
_____
_____

Additional Thoughts:

_____
_____
_____
_____

Day 52

How many hours of sleep did I get last night? _____

Today I'm feeling:

Exhausted   A bit tired   Refreshed   Like I can climb a mountain

Overall, I'm feeling:

Excited   Joyful   Okay   Overwhelmed   Down   _____

What will I do for me to keep or boost this mood?

_____

Today, I am grateful and happy for:

1. _____
2. _____
3. _____

My desires and goals for today:

_____
_____
_____
_____
_____
_____
_____

Today is: __ / __ / __

Today's challenges and/or what I am most proud of:

_____
_____
_____
_____
_____
_____

Who/what brought me joy, helped, or made me smile? _____

_____

Who did I show gratitude to today, and why? _____

_____

Tomorrow's Top Three Goals:

_____
_____
_____

Additional Thoughts:

_____
_____
_____
_____
_____

Day 53

How many hours of sleep did I get last night? _____

Today I'm feeling:

Exhausted   A bit tired   Refreshed   Like I can climb a mountain

Overall, I'm feeling:

Excited   Joyful   Okay   Overwhelmed   Down   _____

What will I do for me to keep or boost this mood?
_____

Today, I am grateful and happy for:

1. _____
2. _____
3. _____

My desires and goals for today:

_____
_____
_____
_____
_____
_____
_____

Today is: __ / __ / __

Today's challenges and/or what I am most proud of:

_____
_____
_____
_____
_____
_____

Who/what brought me joy, helped, or made me smile? _____

_____

Who did I show gratitude to today, and why? _____

_____

Tomorrow's Top Three Goals:

_____
_____
_____

Additional Thoughts:

_____
_____
_____
_____

Day 54

How many hours of sleep did I get last night? _____

Today I'm feeling:

Exhausted   A bit tired   Refreshed   Like I can climb a mountain

Overall, I'm feeling:

Excited   Joyful   Okay   Overwhelmed   Down   _____

What will I do for me to keep or boost this mood?

_____

Today, I am grateful and happy for:

1. _____
2. _____
3. _____

My desires and goals for today:

_____
_____
_____
_____
_____
_____
_____

Today is: __ / __ / __

Today's challenges and/or what I am most proud of:

_____
_____
_____
_____
_____
_____

Who/what brought me joy, helped, or made me smile? _____

_____

Who did I show gratitude to today, and why? _____

_____

Tomorrow's Top Three Goals:

_____
_____
_____

Additional Thoughts:

_____
_____
_____
_____
_____

Day 55

How many hours of sleep did I get last night? _____

Today I'm feeling:

Exhausted   A bit tired   Refreshed   Like I can climb a mountain

Overall, I'm feeling:

Excited   Joyful   Okay   Overwhelmed   Down   _____

What will I do for me to keep or boost this mood?

_____

Today, I am grateful and happy for:

1. _____
2. _____
3. _____

My desires and goals for today:

_____
_____
_____
_____
_____
_____
_____
_____

Today is: __ / __ / __

Today's challenges and/or what I am most proud of:

_____
_____
_____
_____
_____
_____

Who/what brought me joy, helped, or made me smile? _____

_____

Who did I show gratitude to today, and why? _____

_____

Tomorrow's Top Three Goals:

_____
_____
_____

Additional Thoughts:

_____
_____
_____
_____
_____

Day 56

How many hours of sleep did I get last night? _____

Today I'm feeling:

Exhausted   A bit tired   Refreshed   Like I can climb a mountain

Overall, I'm feeling:

Excited   Joyful   Okay   Overwhelmed   Down   _____

What will I do for me to keep or boost this mood?

_____

Today, I am grateful and happy for:

1. _____
2. _____
3. _____

My desires and goals for today:

_____
_____
_____
_____
_____
_____
_____

Today is: __ / __ / __

Today's challenges and/or what I am most proud of:

_____
_____
_____
_____
_____
_____

Who/what brought me joy, helped, or made me smile? _____

_____

Who did I show gratitude to today, and why? _____

_____

Tomorrow's Top Three Goals:

_____
_____
_____

Additional Thoughts:

_____
_____
_____
_____
_____

Day 57

How many hours of sleep did I get last night? _____

Today I'm feeling:

Exhausted   A bit tired   Refreshed   Like I can climb a mountain

Overall, I'm feeling:

Excited   Joyful   Okay   Overwhelmed   Down   _____

What will I do for me to keep or boost this mood?

_____

Today, I am grateful and happy for:

1. _____
2. _____
3. _____

My desires and goals for today:

_____

_____

_____

_____

_____

_____

_____

Today is: __ / __ / __

Today's challenges and/or what I am most proud of:

_____
_____
_____
_____
_____
_____

Who/what brought me joy, helped, or made me smile? _____

_____

Who did I show gratitude to today, and why? _____

_____

Tomorrow's Top Three Goals:

_____
_____
_____

Additional Thoughts:

_____
_____
_____
_____
_____

Day 58

How many hours of sleep did I get last night? _____

Today I'm feeling:

Exhausted   A bit tired   Refreshed   Like I can climb a mountain

Overall, I'm feeling:

Excited   Joyful   Okay   Overwhelmed   Down   _____

What will I do for me to keep or boost this mood?
_____

Today, I am grateful and happy for:

1. _____
2. _____
3. _____

My desires and goals for today:
_____
_____
_____
_____
_____
_____
_____

Today is: __ / __ / __

Today's challenges and/or what I am most proud of:

_____
_____
_____
_____
_____
_____

Who/what brought me joy, helped, or made me smile? _____

_____

Who did I show gratitude to today, and why? _____

_____

Tomorrow's Top Three Goals:

_____
_____
_____

Additional Thoughts:

_____
_____
_____
_____
_____

Day 59

How many hours of sleep did I get last night? _____

Today I'm feeling:

Exhausted   A bit tired   Refreshed   Like I can climb a mountain

Overall, I'm feeling:

Excited   Joyful   Okay   Overwhelmed   Down   _____

What will I do for me to keep or boost this mood?

_____

Today, I am grateful and happy for:

1. _____
2. _____
3. _____

My desires and goals for today:

_____
_____
_____
_____
_____
_____
_____

Today is: __ / __ / __

Today's challenges and/or what I am most proud of:

_____
_____
_____
_____
_____
_____

Who/what brought me joy, helped, or made me smile? _____

_____

Who did I show gratitude to today, and why? _____

_____

Tomorrow's Top Three Goals:

_____
_____
_____

Additional Thoughts:

_____
_____
_____
_____
_____

Day 60

How many hours of sleep did I get last night? _____

Today I'm feeling:

Exhausted   A bit tired   Refreshed   Like I can climb a mountain

Overall, I'm feeling:

Excited   Joyful   Okay   Overwhelmed   Down   _____

What will I do for me to keep or boost this mood?

_____

Today, I am grateful and happy for:

1. _____
2. _____
3. _____

My desires and goals for today:

_____
_____
_____
_____
_____
_____
_____

Today is: __ / __ / __

Today's challenges and/or what I am most proud of:

_____
_____
_____
_____
_____
_____

Who/what brought me joy, helped, or made me smile? _____

_____

Who did I show gratitude to today, and why? _____

_____

Tomorrow's Top Three Goals:

_____
_____
_____

Additional Thoughts:

_____
_____
_____
_____

Day 61

How many hours of sleep did I get last night? _____

Today I'm feeling:

Exhausted   A bit tired   Refreshed   Like I can climb a mountain

Overall, I'm feeling:

Excited   Joyful   Okay   Overwhelmed   Down   _____

What will I do for me to keep or boost this mood?

_____

Today, I am grateful and happy for:

1. _____
2. _____
3. _____

My desires and goals for today:

_____
_____
_____
_____
_____
_____
_____
_____

Today is: __ / __ / __

Today's challenges and/or what I am most proud of:

_____
_____
_____
_____
_____
_____

Who/what brought me joy, helped, or made me smile? _____

_____

Who did I show gratitude to today, and why? _____

_____

Tomorrow's Top Three Goals:

_____
_____
_____

Additional Thoughts:

_____
_____
_____
_____

Day 62

How many hours of sleep did I get last night? _____

Today I'm feeling:

Exhausted   A bit tired   Refreshed   Like I can climb a mountain

Overall, I'm feeling:

Excited   Joyful   Okay   Overwhelmed   Down   _____

What will I do for me to keep or boost this mood?

_____

Today, I am grateful and happy for:

1. _____
2. _____
3. _____

My desires and goals for today:

_____
_____
_____
_____
_____
_____
_____

Today is: __ / __ / __

Today's challenges and/or what I am most proud of:

_____
_____
_____
_____
_____
_____

Who/what brought me joy, helped, or made me smile? _____

_____

Who did I show gratitude to today, and why? _____

_____

Tomorrow's Top Three Goals:

_____
_____
_____

Additional Thoughts:

_____
_____
_____
_____
_____

Day 63

How many hours of sleep did I get last night? _____

Today I'm feeling:

Exhausted   A bit tired   Refreshed   Like I can climb a mountain

Overall, I'm feeling:

Excited   Joyful   Okay   Overwhelmed   Down   _____

What will I do for me to keep or boost this mood?

_____

Today, I am grateful and happy for:

1. _____
2. _____
3. _____

My desires and goals for today:

_____
_____
_____
_____
_____
_____
_____

Today is: __ / __ / __

Today's challenges and/or what I am most proud of:

_____
_____
_____
_____
_____
_____

Who/what brought me joy, helped, or made me smile? _____

_____

Who did I show gratitude to today, and why? _____

_____

Tomorrow's Top Three Goals:

_____
_____
_____

Additional Thoughts:

_____
_____
_____
_____
_____

Day 64

How many hours of sleep did I get last night? _____

Today I'm feeling:

Exhausted   A bit tired   Refreshed   Like I can climb a mountain

Overall, I'm feeling:

Excited   Joyful   Okay   Overwhelmed   Down   _____

What will I do for me to keep or boost this mood?

_____

Today, I am grateful and happy for:

1. _____
2. _____
3. _____

My desires and goals for today:

_____
_____
_____
_____
_____
_____
_____
_____

Today is: __ / __ / __

Today's challenges and/or what I am most proud of:

_____
_____
_____
_____
_____
_____

Who/what brought me joy, helped, or made me smile? _____

_____

Who did I show gratitude to today, and why? _____

_____

Tomorrow's Top Three Goals:

_____
_____
_____

Additional Thoughts:

_____
_____
_____
_____
_____

Day 65

How many hours of sleep did I get last night? _____

Today I'm feeling:

Exhausted   A bit tired   Refreshed   Like I can climb a mountain

Overall, I'm feeling:

Excited   Joyful   Okay   Overwhelmed   Down   _____

What will I do for me to keep or boost this mood?

_____

Today, I am grateful and happy for:

1. _____
2. _____
3. _____

My desires and goals for today:

_____
_____
_____
_____
_____
_____
_____

Today is: __/__/__

Today's challenges and/or what I am most proud of:

_____
_____
_____
_____
_____
_____

Who/what brought me joy, helped, or made me smile? _____

_____

Who did I show gratitude to today, and why? _____

_____

Tomorrow's Top Three Goals:

_____
_____
_____

Additional Thoughts:

_____
_____
_____
_____
_____

Day 66

How many hours of sleep did I get last night? _____

Today I'm feeling:

Exhausted   A bit tired   Refreshed   Like I can climb a mountain

Overall, I'm feeling:

Excited   Joyful   Okay   Overwhelmed   Down   _____

What will I do for me to keep or boost this mood?

_____

Today, I am grateful and happy for:

1. _____
2. _____
3. _____

My desires and goals for today:

_____
_____
_____
_____
_____
_____
_____

Today is: __ / __ / __

Today's challenges and/or what I am most proud of:

_____

_____

_____

_____

_____

Who/what brought me joy, helped, or made me smile? _____

_____

Who did I show gratitude to today, and why? _____

_____

Tomorrow's Top Three Goals:

_____

_____

_____

Additional Thoughts:

_____

_____

_____

_____

_____

Day 67

How many hours of sleep did I get last night? _____

Today I'm feeling:

Exhausted   A bit tired   Refreshed   Like I can climb a mountain

Overall, I'm feeling:

Excited   Joyful   Okay   Overwhelmed   Down   _____

What will I do for me to keep or boost this mood?

_____

Today, I am grateful and happy for:

1. _____
2. _____
3. _____

My desires and goals for today:

_____
_____
_____
_____
_____
_____
_____

Today is: __ / __ / __

Today's challenges and/or what I am most proud of:

_____
_____
_____
_____
_____
_____

Who/what brought me joy, helped, or made me smile? _____

_____

Who did I show gratitude to today, and why? _____

_____

Tomorrow's Top Three Goals:

_____
_____
_____

Additional Thoughts:

_____
_____
_____
_____

Day 68

How many hours of sleep did I get last night? _____

Today I'm feeling:

Exhausted   A bit tired   Refreshed   Like I can climb a mountain

Overall, I'm feeling:

Excited   Joyful   Okay   Overwhelmed   Down   _____

What will I do for me to keep or boost this mood?

_____

Today, I am grateful and happy for:

1. _____
2. _____
3. _____

My desires and goals for today:

_____
_____
_____
_____
_____
_____
_____

Today is: __ / __ / __

Today's challenges and/or what I am most proud of:

___

___

___

___

___

___

Who/what brought me joy, helped, or made me smile? ___

___

Who did I show gratitude to today, and why? ___

___

Tomorrow's Top Three Goals:

___

___

___

Additional Thoughts:

___

___

___

___

___

Day 69

How many hours of sleep did I get last night? _____

Today I'm feeling:

Exhausted   A bit tired   Refreshed   Like I can climb a mountain

Overall, I'm feeling:

Excited   Joyful   Okay   Overwhelmed   Down   _____

What will I do for me to keep or boost this mood?
_____

Today, I am grateful and happy for:

1. _____
2. _____
3. _____

My desires and goals for today:

_____
_____
_____
_____
_____
_____
_____

Today is: __ / __ / __

Today's challenges and/or what I am most proud of:

_____
_____
_____
_____
_____
_____

Who/what brought me joy, helped, or made me smile? _____

_____

Who did I show gratitude to today, and why? _____

_____

Tomorrow's Top Three Goals:

_____
_____
_____

Additional Thoughts:

_____
_____
_____
_____
_____

Day 70

How many hours of sleep did I get last night? _____

Today I'm feeling:

Exhausted   A bit tired   Refreshed   Like I can climb a mountain

Overall, I'm feeling:

Excited   Joyful   Okay   Overwhelmed   Down   _____

What will I do for me to keep or boost this mood?

_____

Today, I am grateful and happy for:

1. _____
2. _____
3. _____

My desires and goals for today:

_____
_____
_____
_____
_____
_____
_____
_____

Today is: __ / __ / __

Today's challenges and/or what I am most proud of:

_____
_____
_____
_____
_____

Who/what brought me joy, helped, or made me smile? _____

_____

Who did I show gratitude to today, and why? _____

_____

Tomorrow's Top Three Goals:

_____
_____
_____

Additional Thoughts:

_____
_____
_____
_____

Day 71

How many hours of sleep did I get last night? _____

Today I'm feeling:

Exhausted   A bit tired   Refreshed   Like I can climb a mountain

Overall, I'm feeling:

Excited   Joyful   Okay   Overwhelmed   Down   _____

What will I do for me to keep or boost this mood?

_____

Today, I am grateful and happy for:

1. _____
2. _____
3. _____

My desires and goals for today:

_____

_____

_____

_____

_____

_____

_____

Today is: __ / __ / __

Today's challenges and/or what I am most proud of:

_____

_____

_____

_____

_____

_____

Who/what brought me joy, helped, or made me smile? _____

_____

Who did I show gratitude to today, and why? _____

_____

Tomorrow's Top Three Goals:

_____

_____

_____

Additional Thoughts:

_____

_____

_____

_____

_____

Day 72

How many hours of sleep did I get last night? _____

Today I'm feeling:

Exhausted   A bit tired   Refreshed   Like I can climb a mountain

Overall, I'm feeling:

Excited   Joyful   Okay   Overwhelmed   Down   _____

What will I do for me to keep or boost this mood?

_____

Today, I am grateful and happy for:

1. _____
2. _____
3. _____

My desires and goals for today:

_____
_____
_____
_____
_____
_____
_____

Today is: __ / __ / __

Today's challenges and/or what I am most proud of:

_____
_____
_____
_____
_____
_____

Who/what brought me joy, helped, or made me smile? _____

_____

Who did I show gratitude to today, and why? _____

_____

Tomorrow's Top Three Goals:

_____
_____
_____

Additional Thoughts:

_____
_____
_____
_____
_____

Day 73

How many hours of sleep did I get last night? _____

Today I'm feeling:

Exhausted   A bit tired   Refreshed   Like I can climb a mountain

Overall, I'm feeling:

Excited   Joyful   Okay   Overwhelmed   Down   _____

What will I do for me to keep or boost this mood?

_____

Today, I am grateful and happy for:

1. _____
2. _____
3. _____

My desires and goals for today:

_____
_____
_____
_____
_____
_____
_____
_____

Today is: __ / __ / __

Today's challenges and/or what I am most proud of:

_____
_____
_____
_____
_____
_____

Who/what brought me joy, helped, or made me smile? _____

_____

Who did I show gratitude to today, and why? _____

_____

Tomorrow's Top Three Goals:

_____
_____
_____

Additional Thoughts:

_____
_____
_____
_____
_____

Day 74

How many hours of sleep did I get last night? _____

Today I'm feeling:

Exhausted   A bit tired   Refreshed   Like I can climb a mountain

Overall, I'm feeling:

Excited   Joyful   Okay   Overwhelmed   Down   _____

What will I do for me to keep or boost this mood?

_____

Today, I am grateful and happy for:

1. _____
2. _____
3. _____

My desires and goals for today:

_____
_____
_____
_____
_____
_____
_____

Today is: __ / __ / __

Today's challenges and/or what I am most proud of:

_____
_____
_____
_____
_____
_____

Who/what brought me joy, helped, or made me smile? _____

_____

Who did I show gratitude to today, and why? _____

_____

Tomorrow's Top Three Goals:

_____
_____
_____

Additional Thoughts:

_____
_____
_____
_____
_____

Day 75

How many hours of sleep did I get last night? _____

Today I'm feeling:

Exhausted   A bit tired   Refreshed   Like I can climb a mountain

Overall, I'm feeling:

Excited   Joyful   Okay   Overwhelmed   Down   _____

What will I do for me to keep or boost this mood?

_____

Today, I am grateful and happy for:

1. _____
2. _____
3. _____

My desires and goals for today:

_____
_____
_____
_____
_____
_____
_____

Today is: __ / __ / __

Today's challenges and/or what I am most proud of:

_____
_____
_____
_____
_____
_____

Who/what brought me joy, helped, or made me smile? _____

_____

Who did I show gratitude to today, and why? _____

_____

Tomorrow's Top Three Goals:

_____
_____
_____

Additional Thoughts:

_____
_____
_____
_____
_____

Day 76

How many hours of sleep did I get last night? _____

Today I'm feeling:

Exhausted   A bit tired   Refreshed   Like I can climb a mountain

Overall, I'm feeling:

Excited   Joyful   Okay   Overwhelmed   Down   _____

What will I do for me to keep or boost this mood?

_____

Today, I am grateful and happy for:

1. _____
2. _____
3. _____

My desires and goals for today:

_____
_____
_____
_____
_____
_____
_____

Today is: __ / __ / __

Today's challenges and/or what I am most proud of:

_____
_____
_____
_____
_____
_____
_____

Who/what brought me joy, helped, or made me smile? _____

_____

Who did I show gratitude to today, and why? _____

_____

Tomorrow's Top Three Goals:

_____
_____
_____

Additional Thoughts:

_____
_____
_____
_____
_____

Day 77

How many hours of sleep did I get last night? _____

Today I'm feeling:

Exhausted   A bit tired   Refreshed   Like I can climb a mountain

Overall, I'm feeling:

Excited   Joyful   Okay   Overwhelmed   Down   _____

What will I do for me to keep or boost this mood?

_____

Today, I am grateful and happy for:

1. _____
2. _____
3. _____

My desires and goals for today:

_____
_____
_____
_____
_____
_____
_____

Today is: __ / __ / __

Today's challenges and/or what I am most proud of:

_____
_____
_____
_____
_____
_____

Who/what brought me joy, helped, or made me smile? _____

_____

Who did I show gratitude to today, and why? _____

_____

Tomorrow's Top Three Goals:

_____
_____
_____

Additional Thoughts:

_____
_____
_____
_____
_____

Day 78

How many hours of sleep did I get last night? _____

Today I'm feeling:

Exhausted   A bit tired   Refreshed   Like I can climb a mountain

Overall, I'm feeling:

Excited   Joyful   Okay   Overwhelmed   Down   _____

What will I do for me to keep or boost this mood?

_____

Today, I am grateful and happy for:

1. _____
2. _____
3. _____

My desires and goals for today:

_____
_____
_____
_____
_____
_____
_____

Today is: __ / __ / __

Today's challenges and/or what I am most proud of:

_____
_____
_____
_____
_____
_____

Who/what brought me joy, helped, or made me smile? _____

_____

Who did I show gratitude to today, and why? _____

_____

Tomorrow's Top Three Goals:

_____
_____
_____

Additional Thoughts:

_____
_____
_____
_____

Day 79

How many hours of sleep did I get last night? _____

Today I'm feeling:

Exhausted   A bit tired   Refreshed   Like I can climb a mountain

Overall, I'm feeling:

Excited   Joyful   Okay   Overwhelmed   Down   _____

What will I do for me to keep or boost this mood?

_____

Today, I am grateful and happy for:

1. _____
2. _____
3. _____

My desires and goals for today:

_____
_____
_____
_____
_____
_____
_____

Today is: __ /__ /__

Today's challenges and/or what I am most proud of:

_____
_____
_____
_____
_____
_____

Who/what brought me joy, helped, or made me smile? _____

_____

Who did I show gratitude to today, and why? _____

_____

Tomorrow's Top Three Goals:

_____
_____
_____

Additional Thoughts:

_____
_____
_____
_____

Day 80

How many hours of sleep did I get last night? _____

Today I'm feeling:

Exhausted   A bit tired   Refreshed   Like I can climb a mountain

Overall, I'm feeling:

Excited   Joyful   Okay   Overwhelmed   Down   _____

What will I do for me to keep or boost this mood?

_____

Today, I am grateful and happy for:

1. _____
2. _____
3. _____

My desires and goals for today:

_____
_____
_____
_____
_____
_____
_____

Today is: __ / __ / __

Today's challenges and/or what I am most proud of:

_____

_____

_____

_____

_____

_____

Who/what brought me joy, helped, or made me smile? _____

_____

Who did I show gratitude to today, and why? _____

_____

Tomorrow's Top Three Goals:

_____

_____

_____

Additional Thoughts:

_____

_____

_____

_____

_____

Day 81

How many hours of sleep did I get last night? _____

Today I'm feeling:

Exhausted   A bit tired   Refreshed   Like I can climb a mountain

Overall, I'm feeling:

Excited   Joyful   Okay   Overwhelmed   Down   _____

What will I do for me to keep or boost this mood?

_____

Today, I am grateful and happy for:

1. _____
2. _____
3. _____

My desires and goals for today:

_____
_____
_____
_____
_____
_____
_____

Today is: __ / __ / __

Today's challenges and/or what I am most proud of:

_____
_____
_____
_____
_____
_____

Who/what brought me joy, helped, or made me smile? _____

_____

Who did I show gratitude to today, and why? _____

_____

Tomorrow's Top Three Goals:

_____
_____
_____

Additional Thoughts:

_____
_____
_____
_____
_____

Day 82

How many hours of sleep did I get last night? _____

Today I'm feeling:

Exhausted   A bit tired   Refreshed   Like I can climb a mountain

Overall, I'm feeling:

Excited   Joyful   Okay   Overwhelmed   Down   _____

What will I do for me to keep or boost this mood?

_____

Today, I am grateful and happy for:

1. _____
2. _____
3. _____

My desires and goals for today:

_____

_____

_____

_____

_____

_____

_____

Today is: __/__/__

Today's challenges and/or what I am most proud of:

_____
_____
_____
_____
_____
_____

Who/what brought me joy, helped, or made me smile? _____

_____

Who did I show gratitude to today, and why? _____

_____

Tomorrow's Top Three Goals:

_____
_____
_____

Additional Thoughts:

_____
_____
_____
_____
_____

Day 83

How many hours of sleep did I get last night? _____

Today I'm feeling:

Exhausted   A bit tired   Refreshed   Like I can climb a mountain

Overall, I'm feeling:

Excited   Joyful   Okay   Overwhelmed   Down   _____

What will I do for me to keep or boost this mood?

_____

Today, I am grateful and happy for:

1. _____
2. _____
3. _____

My desires and goals for today:

_____
_____
_____
_____
_____
_____
_____

Today is: __ / __ / __

Today's challenges and/or what I am most proud of:

___

Who/what brought me joy, helped, or made me smile?

___

Who did I show gratitude to today, and why?

___

Tomorrow's Top Three Goals:

___

Additional Thoughts:

___

Day 84

How many hours of sleep did I get last night? _____

Today I'm feeling:

Exhausted   A bit tired   Refreshed   Like I can climb a mountain

Overall, I'm feeling:

Excited   Joyful   Okay   Overwhelmed   Down   _____

What will I do for me to keep or boost this mood?

_____

Today, I am grateful and happy for:

1. _____
2. _____
3. _____

My desires and goals for today:

_____
_____
_____
_____
_____
_____
_____

Today is: __/__/__

Today's challenges and/or what I am most proud of:

_____
_____
_____
_____
_____

Who/what brought me joy, helped, or made me smile? _____

_____

Who did I show gratitude to today, and why? _____

_____

Tomorrow's Top Three Goals:

_____
_____
_____

Additional Thoughts:

_____
_____
_____
_____

Day 85

How many hours of sleep did I get last night? _____

Today I'm feeling:

Exhausted   A bit tired   Refreshed   Like I can climb a mountain

Overall, I'm feeling:

Excited   Joyful   Okay   Overwhelmed   Down   _____

What will I do for me to keep or boost this mood?

_____

Today, I am grateful and happy for:

1. _____
2. _____
3. _____

My desires and goals for today:

_____
_____
_____
_____
_____
_____
_____
_____

Today is: __ / __ / __

Today's challenges and/or what I am most proud of:

_____
_____
_____
_____
_____
_____

Who/what brought me joy, helped, or made me smile? _____

_____

Who did I show gratitude to today, and why? _____

_____

Tomorrow's Top Three Goals:

_____
_____
_____

Additional Thoughts:

_____
_____
_____
_____
_____

Day 86

How many hours of sleep did I get last night? _____

Today I'm feeling:

Exhausted   A bit tired   Refreshed   Like I can climb a mountain

Overall, I'm feeling:

Excited   Joyful   Okay   Overwhelmed   Down   _____

What will I do for me to keep or boost this mood?

_____

Today, I am grateful and happy for:

1. _____
2. _____
3. _____

My desires and goals for today:

_____
_____
_____
_____
_____
_____
_____
_____

Today is: __ / __ / __

Today's challenges and/or what I am most proud of:

_____
_____
_____
_____
_____
_____

Who/what brought me joy, helped, or made me smile? _____

_____

Who did I show gratitude to today, and why? _____

_____

Tomorrow's Top Three Goals:

_____
_____
_____

Additional Thoughts:

_____
_____
_____
_____
_____

Day 87

How many hours of sleep did I get last night? _____

Today I'm feeling:

Exhausted   A bit tired   Refreshed   Like I can climb a mountain

Overall, I'm feeling:

Excited   Joyful   Okay   Overwhelmed   Down   _____

What will I do for me to keep or boost this mood?

_____

Today, I am grateful and happy for:

1. _____
2. _____
3. _____

My desires and goals for today:

_____

_____

_____

_____

_____

_____

_____

Today is: __ / __ / __

Today's challenges and/or what I am most proud of:

_____
_____
_____
_____
_____
_____

Who/what brought me joy, helped, or made me smile? _____

_____

Who did I show gratitude to today, and why? _____

_____

Tomorrow's Top Three Goals:

_____
_____
_____

Additional Thoughts:

_____
_____
_____
_____
_____

Day 88

How many hours of sleep did I get last night? _____

Today I'm feeling:

Exhausted   A bit tired   Refreshed   Like I can climb a mountain

Overall, I'm feeling:

Excited   Joyful   Okay   Overwhelmed   Down   _____

What will I do for me to keep or boost this mood?
_____

Today, I am grateful and happy for:

1. _____
2. _____
3. _____

My desires and goals for today:

_____
_____
_____
_____
_____
_____
_____

Today is: __/__/__

Today's challenges and/or what I am most proud of:

_____
_____
_____
_____
_____

Who/what brought me joy, helped, or made me smile? _____

_____

Who did I show gratitude to today, and why? _____

_____

Tomorrow's Top Three Goals:

_____
_____
_____

Additional Thoughts:

_____
_____
_____
_____
_____

Day 89

How many hours of sleep did I get last night? _____

Today I'm feeling:

Exhausted   A bit tired   Refreshed   Like I can climb a mountain

Overall, I'm feeling:

Excited   Joyful   Okay   Overwhelmed   Down   _____

What will I do for me to keep or boost this mood?

_____

Today, I am grateful and happy for:

1. _____
2. _____
3. _____

My desires and goals for today:

_____
_____
_____
_____
_____
_____
_____
_____

Today is: __ / __ / __

Today's challenges and/or what I am most proud of:

_____
_____
_____
_____
_____
_____

Who/what brought me joy, helped, or made me smile? _____

_____

Who did I show gratitude to today, and why? _____

_____

Tomorrow's Top Three Goals:

_____
_____
_____

Additional Thoughts:

_____
_____
_____
_____
_____

Day 90

How many hours of sleep did I get last night? _____

Today I'm feeling:

Exhausted   A bit tired   Refreshed   Like I can climb a mountain

Overall, I'm feeling:

Excited   Joyful   Okay   Overwhelmed   Down   _____

What will I do for me to keep or boost this mood?

_____

Today, I am grateful and happy for:

1. _____
2. _____
3. _____

My desires and goals for today:

_____

_____

_____

_____

_____

_____

_____

Today is: __ / __ / __

Today's challenges and/or what I am most proud of:

_____
_____
_____
_____
_____
_____

Who/what brought me joy, helped, or made me smile? _____
_____

Who did I show gratitude to today, and why? _____
_____

Tomorrow's Top Three Goals:

_____
_____
_____

Additional Thoughts:

_____
_____
_____
_____
_____

Day 91

How many hours of sleep did I get last night? _____

Today I'm feeling:

Exhausted   A bit tired   Refreshed   Like I can climb a mountain

Overall, I'm feeling:

Excited   Joyful   Okay   Overwhelmed   Down   _____

What will I do for me to keep or boost this mood?

_____

Today, I am grateful and happy for:

1. _____
2. _____
3. _____

My desires and goals for today:

_____
_____
_____
_____
_____
_____
_____

Today is: __ / __ / __

Today's challenges and/or what I am most proud of:

_____
_____
_____
_____
_____
_____

Who/what brought me joy, helped, or made me smile? _____

_____

Who did I show gratitude to today, and why? _____

_____

Tomorrow's Top Three Goals:

_____
_____
_____

Additional Thoughts:

_____
_____
_____
_____
_____

Day 92

How many hours of sleep did I get last night? _____

Today I'm feeling:

Exhausted   A bit tired   Refreshed   Like I can climb a mountain

Overall, I'm feeling:

Excited   Joyful   Okay   Overwhelmed   Down   _____

What will I do for me to keep or boost this mood?

_____

Today, I am grateful and happy for:

1. _____
2. _____
3. _____

My desires and goals for today:

_____
_____
_____
_____
_____
_____
_____

Today is: __ / __ / __

Today's challenges and/or what I am most proud of:

_____
_____
_____
_____
_____
_____

Who/what brought me joy, helped, or made me smile? _____

_____

Who did I show gratitude to today, and why? _____

_____

Tomorrow's Top Three Goals:

_____
_____
_____

Additional Thoughts:

_____
_____
_____
_____
_____

Day 93

How many hours of sleep did I get last night? _____

Today I'm feeling:

Exhausted   A bit tired   Refreshed   Like I can climb a mountain

Overall, I'm feeling:

Excited   Joyful   Okay   Overwhelmed   Down   _____

What will I do for me to keep or boost this mood?

_____

Today, I am grateful and happy for:

1. _____
2. _____
3. _____

My desires and goals for today:

_____
_____
_____
_____
_____
_____
_____

Today is: __ / __ / __

Today's challenges and/or what I am most proud of:

_____
_____
_____
_____
_____
_____

Who/what brought me joy, helped, or made me smile? _____

_____

Who did I show gratitude to today, and why? _____

_____

Tomorrow's Top Three Goals:

_____
_____
_____

Additional Thoughts:

_____
_____
_____
_____
_____

Day 94

How many hours of sleep did I get last night? _____

Today I'm feeling:

Exhausted   A bit tired   Refreshed   Like I can climb a mountain

Overall, I'm feeling:

Excited   Joyful   Okay   Overwhelmed   Down   _____

What will I do for me to keep or boost this mood?

_____

Today, I am grateful and happy for:

1. _____
2. _____
3. _____

My desires and goals for today:

_____
_____
_____
_____
_____
_____
_____
_____

Today is: __ / __ / __

Today's challenges and/or what I am most proud of:

_____
_____
_____
_____
_____
_____

Who/what brought me joy, helped, or made me smile? _____

_____

Who did I show gratitude to today, and why? _____

_____

Tomorrow's Top Three Goals:

_____
_____
_____

Additional Thoughts:

_____
_____
_____
_____

Day 95

How many hours of sleep did I get last night? _____

Today I'm feeling:

Exhausted   A bit tired   Refreshed   Like I can climb a mountain

Overall, I'm feeling:

Excited   Joyful   Okay   Overwhelmed   Down   _____

What will I do for me to keep or boost this mood?

_____

Today, I am grateful and happy for:

1. _____
2. _____
3. _____

My desires and goals for today:

_____
_____
_____
_____
_____
_____
_____

Today is: __ / __ / __

Today's challenges and/or what I am most proud of:

_____
_____
_____
_____
_____
_____

Who/what brought me joy, helped, or made me smile? _____

_____

Who did I show gratitude to today, and why? _____

_____

Tomorrow's Top Three Goals:

_____
_____
_____

Additional Thoughts:

_____
_____
_____
_____

_____

Day 96

How many hours of sleep did I get last night? _____

Today I'm feeling:

Exhausted   A bit tired   Refreshed   Like I can climb a mountain

Overall, I'm feeling:

Excited   Joyful   Okay   Overwhelmed   Down   _____

What will I do for me to keep or boost this mood?
_____

Today, I am grateful and happy for:

1. _____
2. _____
3. _____

My desires and goals for today:

_____
_____
_____
_____
_____
_____
_____
_____

Today is: __ / __ / __

Today's challenges and/or what I am most proud of:

_____
_____
_____
_____
_____
_____

Who/what brought me joy, helped, or made me smile? _____

_____

Who did I show gratitude to today, and why? _____

_____

Tomorrow's Top Three Goals:

_____
_____
_____

Additional Thoughts:

_____
_____
_____
_____
_____

Day 97

How many hours of sleep did I get last night? _____

Today I'm feeling:

Exhausted   A bit tired   Refreshed   Like I can climb a mountain

Overall, I'm feeling:

Excited   Joyful   Okay   Overwhelmed   Down   _____

What will I do for me to keep or boost this mood?

_____

Today, I am grateful and happy for:

1. _____
2. _____
3. _____

My desires and goals for today:

_____
_____
_____
_____
_____
_____
_____

Today is: __ / __ / __

Today's challenges and/or what I am most proud of:

_____
_____
_____
_____
_____
_____

Who/what brought me joy, helped, or made me smile? _____

_____

Who did I show gratitude to today, and why? _____

_____

Tomorrow's Top Three Goals:

_____
_____
_____

Additional Thoughts:

_____
_____
_____
_____

Day 98

How many hours of sleep did I get last night? _____

Today I'm feeling:

Exhausted   A bit tired   Refreshed   Like I can climb a mountain

Overall, I'm feeling:

Excited   Joyful   Okay   Overwhelmed   Down   _____

What will I do for me to keep or boost this mood?

_____

Today, I am grateful and happy for:

1. _____
2. _____
3. _____

My desires and goals for today:

_____
_____
_____
_____
_____
_____
_____
_____

Today is: __ / __ / __

Today's challenges and/or what I am most proud of:

_____
_____
_____
_____
_____
_____

Who/what brought me joy, helped, or made me smile? _____

_____

Who did I show gratitude to today, and why? _____

_____

Tomorrow's Top Three Goals:

_____
_____
_____

Additional Thoughts:

_____
_____
_____
_____
_____

Day 99

How many hours of sleep did I get last night? _____

Today I'm feeling:

Exhausted   A bit tired   Refreshed   Like I can climb a mountain

Overall, I'm feeling:

Excited   Joyful   Okay   Overwhelmed   Down   _____

What will I do for me to keep or boost this mood?

_____

Today, I am grateful and happy for:

1. _____
2. _____
3. _____

My desires and goals for today:

_____
_____
_____
_____
_____
_____
_____
_____

Today is: __ / __ / __

Today's challenges and/or what I am most proud of:

_____
_____
_____
_____
_____
_____

Who/what brought me joy, helped, or made me smile? _____

_____

Who did I show gratitude to today, and why? _____

_____

Tomorrow's Top Three Goals:

_____
_____
_____

Additional Thoughts:

_____
_____
_____
_____
_____

Day 100

How many hours of sleep did I get last night? _____

Today I'm feeling:

Exhausted   A bit tired   Refreshed   Like I can climb a mountain

Overall, I'm feeling:

Excited   Joyful   Okay   Overwhelmed   Down   _____

What will I do for me to keep or boost this mood?

_____

Today, I am grateful and happy for:

1. _____
2. _____
3. _____

My desires and goals for today:

_____
_____
_____
_____
_____
_____
_____

Today is: __/__/__

Today's challenges and/or what I am most proud of:

_____
_____
_____
_____
_____

Who/what brought me joy, helped, or made me smile? _____

_____

Who did I show gratitude to today, and why? _____

_____

Tomorrow's Top Three Goals:

_____
_____
_____

Additional Thoughts:

_____
_____
_____
_____

*I am proud of my
COMMITMENT
to my self-care and
wellbeing.*

100 Days! What a win.

Imagine what you can do next when you set a goal and put your mind to it.

You'll be unstoppable.

Tips to Keep or Boost Your Mood

In addition to gratitude, below are five helpful tips to keep or boost your overall mood and well-being:

1. Breathing: You can practice deep breathing anywhere and anytime. Slow, deep breaths through your nose, holding for a five seconds, and then exhaling slowly through your mouth can activate the body's relaxation response, reducing stress and calming your nervous system. If you need an energy boost, pranayama in yoga can revitalize your body and mind. When you breathe, ensure your stomach expands outward while keeping your shoulders still.

2. Meditation: Meditation promotes mindfulness and inner tranquility. Find a quiet and comfortable space, close your eyes, and focus on your breaths to calm your mind. As thoughts arise, acknowledge them without attachment and gently guide your attention back to your breath. Regular meditation can help you develop a sense of presence and inner peace.

3. Nature: Spending time in natural settings can lower stress, promote relaxation, and improve sleep patterns. Nature's sights, sounds, and smells are soothing to the mind and body, reducing cortisol levels and fostering a sense of calm.

4. Movement: Regular physical activity promotes cardiovascular health, strengthens muscles and bones, and triggers the release of endorphins, the "feel-good" hormones, improving mood and reducing stress and anxiety levels. Take a walk, invest in a mini-trampoline, swim, or take your favorite exercise class to incorporate more movement into your routine.

5. Hydration: Staying hydrated is crucial for overall well-being. Water helps with bodily processes like digestion, regulating body temperature, and maintaining cardiovascular health. Adequate hydration also supports cognitive function and boosts energy levels, skin health, and the immune system. Be sure to drink one ounce for each lb you way.

Remember, caring for yourself is essential for our overall well-being. Give yourself permission to take a few moments each day to recharge and restore. Hugs & physical touch also work♥

Made in the USA
Middletown, DE
08 May 2024